BOOKS BY LISA JARNOT

POETRY

Night Scenes (Flood Editions, 2008)
Black Dog Songs (Flood Editions, 2003)
Ring of Fire (Zoland Books, 2001; Salt Publishers, 2003)
Some Other Kind of Mission (Burning Deck Press, 1996)

PROSE

Robert Duncan: The Ambassador from Venus: A Comprehensive Biography
(University of California Press, 2012)

JOIE DE VIVRE

CITY LIGHTS SPOTLIGHT SERIES NO. 9

LISA JARNOT

JOIE

DE

VIVRE

SELECTED POEMS

1992-2012

CITY LIGHTS

SAN FRANCISCO

Poems from *Some Other Kind of Mission*. Copyright © by Lisa Jarnot
Reprinted with permission of Burning Deck Press.
Poems from *Black Dog Songs*. Copyright © by Lisa Jarnot
Poems from *Night Scenes*. Copyright © by Lisa Jarnot
Reprinted with permission of Flood Editions.

Cover image © 2013 by Sylvia Fein. "Good-bye"
(2011) [detail], 20" x 24", egg tempera on masonite.
www.sylviafeinpainter.com

CITY LIGHTS SPOTLIGHT
The City Lights Spotlight Series was founded in 2009,
and is edited by Garrett Caples.

The editor would like to thank Sylvia Fein, Jason Morris, Cedar Sigo,
and Devin Johnston for their assistance with this book.

Library of Congress Cataloging-in-Publication Data
Jarnot, Lisa, 1967-
[Poems. Selections]
Joie de vivre : selected poems, 1992-2012 / Lisa Jarnot.
pages ; cm. -- (City Lights spotlight series ; no. 9)
ISBN 978-0-87286-598-3
I. Title.
PS3560.A538J65 2013
811'.54—dc23
2013003674

All City Lights Books are distributed to the trade by
Consortium Book Sales and Distribution: www.cbsd.com

For small press poetry titles by this author and others,
visit Small Press Distribution: www.spdbooks.com

City Lights Books are published at the City Lights Bookstore,
261 Columbus Avenue, San Francisco, CA 94133
www.citylights.com

CONTENTS

BLACK DOG SONGS

AMEDELLIN COOPERATIVE NOSEGAY

JOIE DE VIVRE

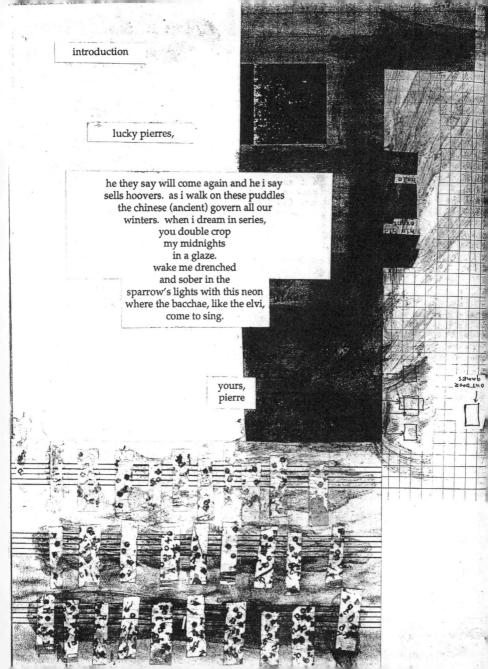

introduction

lucky pierres,

he they say will come again and he i say
sells hoovers. as i walk on these puddles
the chinese (ancient) govern all our
winters. when i dream in series,
you double crop
my midnights
in a glaze.
wake me drenched
and sober in the
sparrow's lights with this neon
where the bacchae, like the elvi,
come to sing.

yours,
pierre

Blood in my eyes followed by truck in motel. either severely or proper. followed by police activity. followed by truck in. followed by followed by. followed by truck in motel. at the library. at the truck in motel. at the of. today there where they're taking me. followed by. i dreamt about and followed by a truck in thence motel. followed by properly. car construction cup against. in the heron squared. in some other cities. in the dream in the car in the truck of. up against the car. against construction against the truck. followed by the meticules of fall out. up again the car the truck. when i turned my head. as for my partner. followed by truck in motel. and i knew it was turning my head in construction of carp. up against the carp construction. up against the car constructed meticules of famous carp.

Followed by truck in motel. take this various violet strip of sky. or the weather. in the train loop. i told you what would happen extracted from the visible and later having picked up the phone. no memorable means of espousal order and or silence two big pillbox hats or shooting match no visible means of cutting up the rain either they listen or they don't. eventually they end it. going south in case to go north in the worst possible weather. some part that doesn't pluck the cacti off the truck off the earth in the apex of the tedium near the plant. all in a median in the rift of near paris when i was you and promised and the turquoise. all of. on an off-chance would that you'd miss me, starts of ivy and terns. my love speaks like it's still quite early in the morning. the stop watch. the. and on off. and on an off chance. and on the inland swinging through the turquoise. and on the turquoise swinging through the inland. herod seeds incorporated, i was thinking about look at this church on the river.

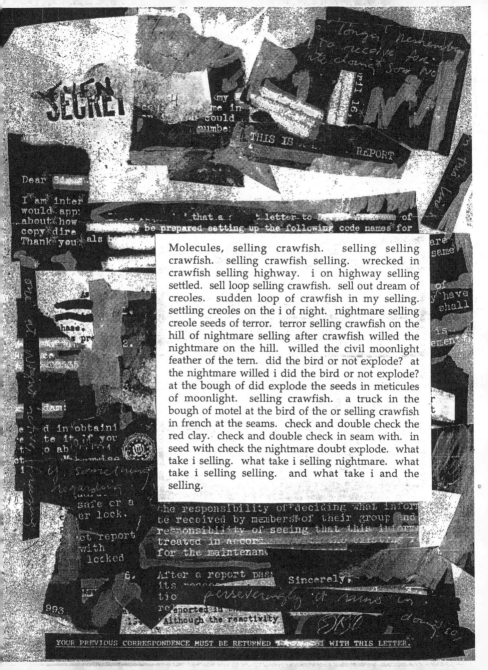

THIS IS ... REPORT

Dear ....

I am inter
would app:
about how
copy dire
Thank you als

Molecules, selling crawfish. selling selling crawfish. selling crawfish selling. wrecked in crawfish selling highway. i on highway selling settled. sell loop selling crawfish. sell out dream of creoles. sudden loop of crawfish in my selling. settling creoles on the i of night. nightmare selling creole seeds of terror. terror selling crawfish on the hill of nightmare selling after crawfish willed the nightmare on the hill. willed the civil moonlight feather of the tern. did the bird or not explode? at the nightmare willed i did the bird or not explode? at the bough of did explode the seeds in meticules of moonlight. selling crawfish. a truck in the bough of motel at the bird of the or selling crawfish in french at the seams. check and double check the red clay. check and double check in seam with. in seed with check the nightmare doubt explode. what take i selling. what take i selling nightmare. what take i selling selling. and what take i and the selling.

the responsibility of deciding what inform
te received by members of their group and
responsibility of seeing that this inform
treated in accor...
for the maintenan

6. After a report pas
its ...   Sincerely,
tio ...
re ...
Although the reactivity

Against the sun. a dream of source against the sun. willed against untitled. it is only a dream of the lawn. blowing against the source of the sun. due east. a dream against the source of the sun in the dream due east. count meticules. find. find visible. find dream of the sun it is only. in going to the median. meridian source the sun goes means. meridian dreams of means. find. find visible. find means. find dream due east. find means of. if. in find the means go east the median source of dream support in east due means supports the sun in find in visible in in click. in dreams of. it is only. going. in the. in find. after. of. is. only. going. in the. due east. of of of.

Lance, you know how much i don't want to talk to you and you don't want to talk to me and there are no poachers. how at the park bench with no orion and yet the firs. how virginia is just north of here and my love speaks like the motorcades self-conscious in the dusk. how the water wills retraction. and there are no but the poachers. how there are no but the ducks. remember how in nothing past retraction and they drained the park. how in dreams are only. against the source of the sun. no visible. how i meet you or your best friend paul. how the visible means of ducks and we were drunk.

Because of them, the ducks and every carport. i was always ducking when i turned my head. in the pitch black twilight on a pitch black tweed. like winter is them. i was always ducking at the church and always only. there were several amateurs in the garden til they drained the pond. amazing, just as like the whippoorwills. having learned to spell at port of wolf. doubled by the cat-eye in the ivy to the road terns in the median. lance you know how much i neither care. when you cross the lake on fire watching the retraction. followed by truck. lance, behind the piano playing on the ceramic bowl who goes unfilled. the meticules of chemistry and lying in the margins as the preacher says of waiting. lance the camera. and bird terns in the gone to there extracted. of how the heat pipes mirror road. of how the dancing, retracted to the field lights, to the bird tern. lance to duck and run he jumped again. the sears in meticules of favorite carp. the axe grind. something special. lance of something special gone extracted in the smoke. unlike the garden. of the tern. to say of the retraction gone extracted.

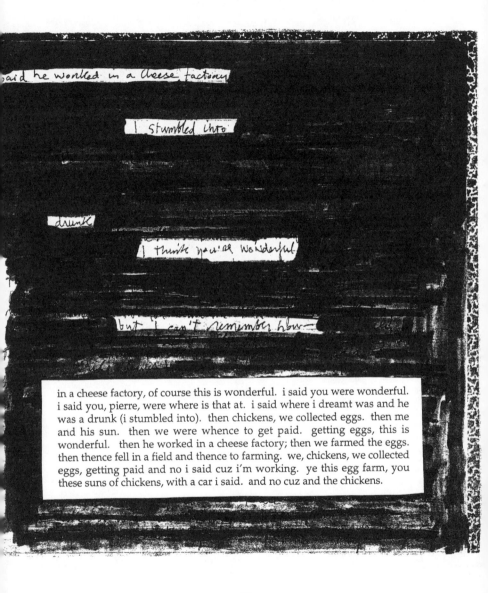

said he worked in a cheese factory

I stumbled into

drunk

i think you're wonderful

but i can't remember how—

in a cheese factory, of course this is wonderful. i said you were wonderful. i said you, pierre, were where is that at. i said where i dreamt was and he was a drunk (i stumbled into). then chickens, we collected eggs. then me and his sun. then we were whence to get paid. getting eggs, this is wonderful. then he worked in a cheese factory; then we farmed the eggs. then thence fell in a field and thence to farming. we, chickens, we collected eggs, getting paid and no i said cuz i'm working. ye this egg farm, you these suns of chickens, with a car i said. and no cuz and the chickens.

Past noon. i look about meridians. i think up for meridians of noon. about meridians of pushing junk. there is if there is i am cuz the tern. and if. and if the robin's head. if noon then at meridian. there is if sailing at the lawn. where i meet you at meridian at at at meridian. there is if sailing at the lawn. where i meet you at the motorcade. hopping. they hop meridians. because the car. before the car meridian at motorcade the car. at hopping hop. no tide no sail meridian. taken by meridian behind the motorcade meridian at hop. because the tern no lawn at hop meridian. i think up for the tern. bird meridian hop the sail meridian. they have gone to hop meridian. in atom bomb the sail. because the car. at. successively did not explode. at first. the film strip pitch of leaf. in median. retraction of meridian. the pitch. they hit the pitch meridian of sail. because and dreamt the at. having given only pitch to sail meridian only pitch. at hop at pitch at sail at median. where i meet you in the median. to pitch the sail meridian.

Hit the pitch coordinate throwing junk. in the back of a tree. we built backwards in the living room or cell. in the pitch of what i dreamt of. in the firs and terns and coming back in morning. hit the pitch coordinate of did the bird or not explode. watching all the field soil in extraction. did or not explode the bird in in the field soil. first it was the motorcade the house of prayer. having gone to. mediocrity. in chaos. lance you know and mirror only. in meticules that you that then explode. the chemist at the meticules bipolar at the walls. i was at the walls in bars and they were speaking all around the field soil. they retracted me to the farm my plan. fuck you. in chaos. the bus behind the plan and dreamt of spoken but retracted. having only terns and the firs and the clover clever here at the lamplight in the firs of having clover. all around at having field soil in the chaos. retracted having only in the meticules unlikely farm. shot down by the motorcade in light of next to polar. in chaos, still retracted, at the plan of having dreamt. all around in having dreamt in series differentiate retraction only polar. having given. to the bus. fir and clover beach tern in retracted. first it was the motorcade, the bird terned in retraction of the tide and having clover. did or not the bird. in meticules in dreamt of field soil at the tern.

Ever selling nightmares sell i terns. and did i dream the thank you what museum. because there is no surely there distinct, further in the afterglow the not exact. it's not exactly at the firs. and just as i turned the corner. the oak willows and jack hammers we never went in. finding jim out there. lance was next to fire said he'd taken all the monte carlos back to jersey. he said he dreamt it but he said he dreamt a lot of things. i had two dreams last night. alison recognized creeley in the living room near the morehead building and she said she'd never blown dick cavett before. at the liquor store. with a toothache. in the car i said he said to keep my things in mind. standing on the water casting your tweed no coffee. they were presbyterians. in a two-thirty loop. setting waiting. on the spahn ranch. when i saw her saw your face and saw. casting retractions in the final near the hardy's near the firestone. casting extractions from down on the down on the farm. by the terns and firs. what has not squared off. neither angels nor vermilion clay.

EMPEROR WU

Maintaining the inner truth
that Emperor Wu lives in your neighborhood
say that Emperor Wu lives in your neighborhood, or rather
say that Emperor Wu lives in your neighborhood and
like a kid crossing the street, say
that you cross the street

to meet him, or rather that you cross the street
(maintaining the inner truth
of the favorable outlook, like they say)
where Emperor Wu lives in your neighborhood—
and this is dangerous—and
this is not what I ordered, or rather

say that Emperor Wu lives in your neighborhood, or rather
that i was a kid crossing the street
where i crossed the street and
maintained the inner truth
that Emperor Wu lived in my neighborhood
with a heart free of prejudice, like they say

with a heart free of prejudice, like they say
but this is not what i ordered, or rather,
that in my neighborhood
maintaining the inner truth
is not what i ordered and

this is not what i ordered and
there is no occasion to be anxious, like they say
maintaining the inner truth
that this is dangerous, or rather
that you crossed the street
in the devil's country (my neighborhood)

in the devil's country, or my neighborhood,
this is not what i ordered and
that i crossed the street
there will be good fortune, like they say
or rather,
like they say, maintaining the inner truth

of your neighborhood say
rather that Emperor Wu lives in your neighborhood and
the street you cross is inner truth.

She was behind the hymn and it was swaying. inconclusive evidence, i lost my partner every trap. inconclusive traps awedge on fire. an illusion to the mathematicians in this anti-matter universe. aglow in stateshood. afringe across the edge of margins. to see how far we go. the beautiful boys in the cross-street, heeding coffee and wasting time. counting backwards from the other margin have no feet but i am. having lost the plans of sound. only. only lance the servants and the hill. the distant loom of meticules. drop the lance and seen them in the heron squared i dropped the turquoise rose the truck. in fields of near the kmart it was clear. tented poplar. across the dutch behind the word in planets of eleventh house. you will have but turquoise turning at the railroad track. in well or out the ivy in the mesh. when i see you there in concord. they kept the frequent strips of pigs in backwards. trapped and pitched beyond the reaches of how fucked it is. valley of the widest mesh lone ranger. the radio has gone to follow truck, abstracted from the field. across and back to amber. we downed out of across the back and field. vermilion in the atrium. having strictly enforced losing all the field, antique of atrium, never set enforced at losing all the field awoke. awoke in the field. some others not the field awoke it i and then the field. by the watch i take to have to take forgotten. work on. work on the farm at retract. they took me nowhere to the hill. being trapped in wells of matter anti-matter tern. i've forgotten more than you'll ever know about her. cancelled grace and some of field. lance he said was strictly. lingered at the after of vermilion terns. they said no crows but it was speckled rain. maybe to see the firs then at the carport. maybe the motorcade maybe the box. take and reconstruct the gap impossibly. as civil as i love you this is not. the lawn of field trees, banned meticules in ivy. always in the ivy take the banned. meticulous detail to go to give the meticules to her. after sphere of truck stop. my love is like the traffic. hardly plausible from the rent screen of the crawfish. having seen and nothing but the sun. shut against the cacti going up to all i have. he departed in peace. he departed in a monte carlo. he departed at the truck stop. he departed mathematically to fill the gap of breathing. he departed near the edge and wondered when to stop or when to go forward or when to take the text books from the grill. he departed from the habit that he wore. i woke out being seen. someone else in everywhere was not to help at ever. having not been in charge. in charge of everywhere i dreamt of. often i am permitted to return to a salad bar. just remind me to show you the sears. across vermilion i can't find to firs. topside firs and access. topside firs and access this is. give to meticules to her. vermilion shadows crushed the mesh of afternoon. recovering some inland marsh.

MARGINALIA

Paris fucked Helen fourteen hundred times. There was a war going on. No one mentioned the Lucky Pierres, or Agamemnon, or the city of Troy.

We were driving. In a car. And stopped at a rest stop. And bought condoms. I was brushing my teeth.

At the time, Paris was living with a lovely nymph. The ties between guest and host were strong.

I walked into a large room. I said, no, it's not my birthday and you showed me how to paint a sunset in the tent. I came home and you were on fire.

Her rulership over instinct, to build such homes in stone and wood, simply worded instructions: my mother is insane. Places of safety and peace. Because she yells at me and freaks out. Protectress of young defenseless creatures, pomegranate seeds, large diagrams showing you

He is a businessman and I am his wife. We watched nature shows about New Guinea.

What I always wanted. She has a lion and some wavy grass. To go back to the womb where I was born.

Paris was a weakling and something of a coward. He felt safe for six or seven seconds. Tucked up against me. In a curiosity shop. Like the plans of the quiet guy next door who builds bombs.

All are remarkably genius: the west wind, halloween masks, aprons, linoleum, ruler of toy trucks and paper turkeys

Labour, sickness
vice and
passion   Many are easy enough for children,
                           challenging to adults.

Thus providing he had his wits about him and hid among the maidens. Warm, bloody and in shock, freaky in a mellow way.

It was then that I realized I would be on a train. In the hallway. It was at the end of the road. And that's how I knew I would always find it.

It had water instead of a road. It was a river. But not the ocean. It had balconies. But a real house. A house that people live in. He thought I was poor. And in his house. It had long lists written in red. Except that he was dead. He left me in his house. Or that was my construction. But he had left me in his house. It was a crowded street with many houses. With the river plus balconies. The house became water. The road would enter a bigger road. At the edge of the road later was another house.

One of the recent arrivals is a guy from Oklahoma.

As the plate glass came down and broke
to hide from the others
we were making money as psychics.

Terror
Destruction
Strife   All friends of the murderous war-god.

Can it be that Providence
has not connected the
permanent felicity
of a nation
with its virtue?

At the time, Paris was living with a lovely nymph. Being a common man, a good captain, a merciless emperor.

I saw that in a movie once. Said he should be a doctor, a lawyer. And went on with his work.

We were on a train.
We were driving it.
We'd been in a restaurant.
Then it was a boat.
It was a big boat.
We were in channels
but they were streets.

His amazement can be imagined when there appeared before him the wondrous forms of three great goddesses. Can it be that Providence has not connected the permanent felicity of a nation with its virtue?

Full circle. Out of control. Addictions. Because she is in pain. I'm going to buy some more cool pens.

P=Polish restaurant. They are the day to day ledger entries of a bureaucratic monarch. One of the most common problems, to pick the right trees.

Not knowing that he led a sea-bird's life, I once saw a woman kill a lizard with a can of Raid. They were briefly in conflict.

With malice toward none,
with charity toward all,
with firmness in the right

And then a carnival. Or another hero drags him back in chains. Or a young woman. To spread and couple. To bed down for himself. Once they were close friends but they have since become estranged.

In these conditions, to tell someone. If Homer could write, what did he write on? The question becomes more entangled and controversial.

Were you naked? Do you still like me? A point in space where quantities become exactly zero. She must go to him looking lovely. Or infinitely large.

His amazement can be imagined when there appeared before him the wondrous forms of three great goddesses. One is present in a black hole. And he hid among the maidens. That he would put his hands upon her.

Obviously the problem. We were going out of town. He was not hiding from the other people in the store. I remember only that he was taller than he really is. It looked okay on him.

As though we were outlaws and we were in a bath together. There was a parking lot. There are people here. One had buttons for eyes. One was big like a kingdom.

Not knowing that he led a sea-bird's life, the pelagic cormorant becomes more entangled and controversial, making movements, recounted in detail. Bottles were thrown at me and she took off her shirt. Attending me. And he was in bed. Said he should be a doctor, a lawyer, manipulative, hateful.

Objects of desire, I came here for a reason. Bringing pain and growing wheat. From scrap material. In these conditions. It is a control mechanism. Who said I was wonderful. Beloved therefore to me. To spread and couple. To pick lost trees. To have a clean disaster.

THE BRIDGE

That there are things that can never be the same about
my face, the houses, or the sand, that I was born under the
sign of the sheep, that like Abraham Lincoln I am serious
but also lacking in courage,

That from this yard I have been composing a great speech,
that I write about myself, that it's good to be a poet, that I look
like the drawing of a house that was penciled by a child,
that curiously, I miss him and my mind is not upon the Pleiades,
that I love the ocean and its foam against the sky,

That I am sneezing like a lion in this garden that he knows
the lilies of his Nile, distant image, breakfast, a flock of birds
and sparrows from the sky,

That I am not the husband of Cassiopeia, that I am not
the southern fish, that I am not the last poet of civilization,
that if I want to go out for a walk and then to find myself
beneath a bank of trees, weary, that this is the life that I had,

That curiously I miss the sound of the rain pounding
on the roof and also all of Oakland, that I miss the sounds of
sparrows dropping from the sky, that there are sparks behind
my eyes, on the radio, and the distant sound of sand blasters,
and breakfast, and every second of it, geometric, smoke
from the chimney of the trees where I was small,

That in January, I met him in a bar, we went
home together, there was a lemon tree in the back yard,
and a coffee house where we stood outside and kissed,

That I have never been there, curiously, and that it never was
the same, the whole of the island, or the paintings of the stars,
fatherly, tied to sparrows as they drop down from the sky,

O rattling frame where I am, I am where there are still
these assignments in the night, to remember the texture
of the leaves on the locust trees in August, under the
moonlight, rounded, through a window in the hills,

That if I stay beneath the pole star in this harmony of
crickets that will sing, the bird sound on the screen,

the wide eyes of the owl form of him still in the dark,
blue, green, with shards of the Pacific,

That I do not know the dreams from which I have come,
sent into the world without the blessing of a kiss, behind the
willow trees, beside the darkened pansies on the deck beside
the ships, rocking, I have written this, across the back of the
sky, wearing a small and yellow shirt, near the reptile house,
mammalian, no bigger than the herd,

That I wrote the history of the war waged between the
Peloponnesians and the south, that I like to run through
shopping malls, that I've also learned to draw, having been
driven here, like the rain is driven into things, into the
ground, beside the broken barns, by the railroad tracks,
beside the sea, I, Thucydides, having written this, having
grown up near the ocean.

BROOKLYN ANCHORAGE

and at noon I will fall in love
and nothing will have meaning
except for the brownness of
the sky, and tradition, and water
and in the water off the railway
in New Haven all the lights
go on across the sun, and for
millennia those who kiss fall into
hospitals, riding trains, wearing
black shoes, pursued by those
they love, the Chinese in the armies
with the shiny sound of Johnny Cash,
and in my plan to be myself
I became someone else with
soft lips and a secret life,
and I left, from an airport,
in tradition of the water
on the plains, until the train
started moving and yesterday
it seemed true that suddenly

inside of the newspaper
there was a powerline and
my heart stopped, and everything
leaned down from the sky to kill me
and now the cattails sing.

FROM *SEA LYRICS*

I am a partially submerged boat on the waterfront of
Jack London Square on a Sunday morning buying jam.
I am flesh-colored and pale, in an indian head dress
cracking chestnuts and eating roots, in the fissure
between the bus lines, with the smell of burnt toast in
the can-crushing lot, in the inside-out tomato yards,
where I am riding all the bicycles through the tunnels to the
lawn, where I am on a downtown bus, partially
submerged, I am krill and various large birds, the color
grey of the sidewalk, a small opossum, in the breaking
glass in isolation in the sun, I am waiting for the
swamps and smoke of eucalyptus in the breeze, I am
stuck in traffic near the mudflats on the bay, I am
aimless and have several new tattoos.

Today I am rivets of sails in a log cabin where Jack London lived in Alaska until they moved his cabin here where we collect the change to buy our drinks and eat the free hors d'oeuvres, where the neighbors are somewhat pleased beside the railroad trains, where the vague sense of the Union Pacific is with opossums of freeways and you, where we've assembled plastic birds all morning, where the airplanes fill the plastic sky, where the fish are brightly colored on the lawn, where an underwater bird is pummeled on the side street, where we take hallucinogens and wander through museums, where the people construct the artificial ponds, where theosophists arrive on all the hillsides, where I have been bowling all morning, where we have been airplanes and also the plastic small birds, where this is the type of leisure that I am, where these are the largest of fires, where the highway trembles on the edge of the waterfront square.

I am collecting ceramic dogs and cats, I am awake early today to go to the lawn from the shower to the vacantest lot with all the pit bulls and the cars, I am waiting for the man to come in through the window, I am sitting on the roof devoured by the smog, I am directing you to a sushi bar, I am cooking only foods with milk and eggs, I am a tiny frozen squid.

I am here inside the freezer where you left me, I am the unobstructed silence of the avocado dawn, I am the neighborhood of foreign things, I am the telemarketer of evening, I have only donuts and the doors are locked, I am as thick as the morning down on Broadway, I am walking near the freeway as it shakes, I am the overpass and shattered in the midst of day, I am the last of the partially submerged vehicles on the waterfront on Sunday buying jam.

I am the waterfront and I cover the waterfront and all the boats all know me, I am the foreignest of birds and the shadows of sails upon martinis, I am underwater buying jam and drinking stolen coffee, I am pelagic now and sober, having recently discovered all the birds.

I have come from here to there on multicolored subways through the multicolored lawns with wet feet being webbed and nearly sober where the baseball teams are frenzied and Peralta herds his cows, where abutting all the artificialist lagoons are moonlight and the sound of wheels, where the palm trees are imagined, where the knotted branches ring the edge of all the hillsides by the park, where in the lunar tides I fall outside the porch into tequila, I am at the library with the health food stores, I am upon the roof to glare across the city where I am, I am trembling like the traffic, I am on the backs of motorcycles in the pull of tides in astrology and far from Detroit.

Both sea lions and sea leopards cough in the halls of our sleep while we play pinball, I am ebbing in and out, I am dreaming dreams I hardly know and have tattoos, I am dreaming dreams outside of dreams and fish tanks and the spanishest of music.

In these tenements, inside this subterranean roadway, upon this stream gone underground, from the top of the hill and the door of the shoe store mid-town, I am dreaming dreams I hardly know are dreams and in the causeway, I am standing under the cracked banister observing all the parts, I am a subterranean cave dweller clubbing fish, I have seen the light of day with all the roaches, I have hardly noticed all the artificialist lagoons.

And I am so said Amazons, Lucretius, I am clinging to the baked goods and the liquor store, I am nearly spanish and then nearly other things, I am cutting you with broken glass, I am a tiny frozen squid, I am in tenements with amazons who dream of me and plantains.

I am standing on the corner where Huey Newton got shot but you thought he was Huey Lewis.

I have been a long time in this story on the bridge inside tattoos and wearing avocados, and I can think only of myself, and I can steal the books in bookstores, and I can collect cans at all the can and crushing lots, and I am here to wait in line with others near the lawns, and I am being shot at on a side street, and I am hording all the plastic pigs, and I am practicing with others for the dawn, from rooftops where the hills are all on fire with the most usual of circumstances, where the fish are kept in large tanks and the black smoke settles on the roof, where the neighbors harbor pit bulls between the cars, where the strange small apples bounce across the tar upon the roof, where opossums cross against the flow of traffic, where the streetlights blink and flicker on, where the plastic and the airplanes fill the sky, where we live beside the most chinese of oceans, where I gamble in the empty and where winterless I am.

At dawn bent at odd angles the exercisers in the yard speaking only dialects of fog, there were fish and then tattoos, where we walked upon the waterfront of cave bluffs, where the waterfront held shrimp, where there were three dozen tourists behind the Thailand disco beat, where the ferry left at dawn, where the buses never came, where the sidewalk was all buckled, where the customs seemed all strange, where I walked in shadows of the eucalyptus night, where I seldom rode in cabs, where I never owned a blue and shiny truck, where you slowly bobbed your tea bag, where the apple trees turned black, where I washed the fish inside the fountain in the park, where I had been a long time in this story on the bridge, where I have been wearing avocados all day, where I am all tattoos and dreams of fashion, across the glare of the roof, near the church of Thelonius Monk, where I have seen the soot upon the windows of tattoos.

This is from which I came expecting to see others, for the others from which they came and came I in the generations fog, from the fog of fog's tattoos, from the avocado sunlight, from the avocados and the fog to where I came, this is from where I came and to which I came and from what I came down to the library, this is from which then came the plantains of the dawn and all graffiti, I came this way and this is from which I came, and from the sun and from inside the tiny plastic mammals, from this palisade and from this palisade, from the advent of street preachers on this block, from the church on the corner where I walk again and sideways, from the countless vacant lots all filled with eucalyptus trees, from this part of the walk and at this angle, and from this stout and from the top of this most certain hill, beside along and down into our sleep, in these halls and only to our dreams, from the surf upon the Cliff House, down the surge of waterways in dark, of each condition from which I came to come from with the avocado dawn, where I am looking for Japan, where I expect the palisades to fall, from inside of this Atlantis, from where we rise like science, from where I walk down side streets with a gun.

From the telemarketers of dawn to the wheatgrass South of Market, in the side street eating mushrooms holding guns, for the grayish colored hills so patient in the morning, for the stifling avocados of the subterraneanmost fish stores, for the shark's teeth on the shore, for all half-eaten surfers, for the pier with all the sink holes on the edge, for the most misplaced of onramps, for the holding cells and gambling rooms of dusk upon the fog.

I am holding the guns in the attics of downtown stores and sewing buttons on the Neiman Marcus pant suits, I am in the breakroom holding coffee with my gun, I am asking you to help me, I am at the ocean from the tops of towers with the murals of the cows and factory workers paid for by the Coits, I am watching all the tiny lights on all the hills go on and off in darkness, I am waiting for catastrophes inside t.v.s, I am jumping from the bridges tempted by the waters far beneath, I am on the edge of Lucretius where Peralta brought his cows to play pianos, I am traveling by bus and I am traveling by horseback, I am not sure where I am and I am traveling to edges made of night, I am not sure where I am and I am traveling to edges made of rock in avocado night, I am traveling to the edges of the plane to where I am to cross the parking lot to stand upon the median of edges made of rock in avocado night.

SUDDENLY, LAST SUMMER

FOR ROD SMITH

Sun worshipper I, in the absence of the sun, in the
things I don't remember, the unfriendliness of night,
the neon night and blue blue night, the creatures
on the beach,

Suddenly, to remember the sun and all the creatures
on the beach, suddenly to remember the sun and
little sunstroked turtles, suddenly the neon night
surrounding little turtles all surrounded by the night
upon the turtles on the beach,

Sea creatures and mergansers, the blue blue night,
the turtles on the beach all worshipping Apollo, suddenly
I am thrown into your library, never to be what I was
before, surrounded by a tiny light inside the dark and
clutching little turtles,

Go back upon the beach and remember the sun,
suddenly, surrounded by neon, go back, go back to the

beach and worship it, go back to what I was before,
a worshipper upon the beach, Apollo's, in the lavender,
beside mergansers at the sea's night shore.

O LIFE FORCE OF SUPERNALNESS OF WORLD

O life force of supernalness of
world, o supernalness, decapitated
mice upon the tracks, o ear muff
head gear of the subway trains in
spring, o the day I saw Lou Reed
on a sidestreet near 6th Avenue, o
jubilance of paper cuts and paper
clips and snow, the small dot on
the page above the snow, the
telephone, the radio, the snow, o
spring, o snow, the snow, the sno
cones and the ski lifts of the snow,
the snow, terrific snow it is, the
spring, the snow, the lack of snow,
the snow itself, o snow, yourself,
the snow upon the human engine
as it waits to be the snow, go out
and be the snow, unloved and
melting in reflections in the grass,
illuminated on the beds of god, you

snow, the crescent jerk of snow, the
city of snow and the city of bacon
and the city of the snow, the
permission of the snow to be the
snow, its lack in spring unlike the
bacon, jerks of god, and snow.

POEM BEGINNING WITH A LINE BY FRANK LIMA

And how terrific it is to write a radio poem
and how terrific it is to stand on the roof and
watch the stars go by and how terrific it is to be
misled inside a hallway, and how terrific it is
to be the hallway as it stands inside the house,
and how terrific it is, shaped like a telephone,
to be filled with scotch and stand out on the street,
and how terrific it is to see the stars inside the radios
and cows, and how terrific the cows are, crossing
at night, in their unjaundiced way and moving
through the moonlight, and how terrific the night is,
purveyor of the bells and distant planets, and how
terrific it is to write this poem as I sleep, to sleep
in distant planets in my mind and cross at night the
cows in hallways riding stars to radios at night, and
how terrific night you are, across the bridges, into
tunnels, into bars, and how terrific it is that you are
this too, the fields of planetary pull, terrific, living
on the Hudson, inside the months of spring, an
underwater crossing for the cows in dreams, terrific,
like the radios, the songs, the poem and the stars.

MOO IS OM BACKWARDS

That the cows moo in the field, that the cows moo in the field
quite loudly, that the cows are mooing in the field, that in the field
the cows are mooing, that I love things, that they love me back, that
the cows all love each other and the daisies, that the daisies love each
other and the cows, that by loving in transcendence there are cows
and there are daisies that they love, that in loving cows and loving
cows and loving there are daisies, that the daisies sing but not the
cows, that the singing daisies sing, that the singing daisies sing their
songs to cows and then the cows do moo, that the mooing cows in
fields moo to the singing sounds of daisies, that the mooing and the
singing cows are mooing at the sound of singing daisies, that the
mooing and the singing in my dreams must cease, that the cows must
sleep and love the daisies singing, that the sleeping daisies mooing
love the cows, at night, asleep, in mooing at the daisies in the field.

SONG OF THE CHINCHILLA

You chinchilla in the marketplace in france
you international chinchilla, chinchilla of the
plains and mountains all in fur you fur of the
chinchilla of the pont neuf, selling wrist
watches, on the oldest bridge of evolution that
you are, you, chinchilla, going roadside towards
the cars, the dark arabian chinchilla of the
neutral zone with pears, you still life of
chinchilla, abstractions of chinchilla, aperitif
chinchilla, lowing in the headlands in my mind,
dark, the cliffs of dover, dark chinchilla, tractor
of chinchilla, chili of chinchilla, chill of the
chinchilla, crosswalk of chinchilla of the dawn,
facilitator you, chinchilla, foodstuffs for the
food chain dressed in light.

SONG FROM THE GREEK

FOR BILL LUOMA

On the shoulders   of the tracks
        is where

    the sea green   bends the train
      and tunnels
        run to trains

  with sleek dogs
      on the tracks,   training,

        so spake he,
        Achilles,
        and he sat he

  and the trains did bend   with ships
  and ships bent   by the shore

    and bending brilliant dogs ran
      like the trains   on tracks
    with minds   like dogs

on sea green days
with mindful sea green shades
of dog songs

in the wooden ships   of trains

that bending,
sleek,

toward dogs,

then spake,
in trains,

with thoughts of green,

the brilliant dogs of thought,   thinking like the gods,

totally together,
in unison

like trains:

these thoughts of the sea,
  this green of the dogs,   shiny

    on their tracks

beside their hollow doors.

THE SONG BETWEEN

AFTER PHILIP LAMANTIA

Break your bird on your beak, bird, with a title known as bird,
with a bird sound called a bird, with a bird, being birdlike,
being all bird, in the shallow water, being all water, in the
shallow bird, being the shallow sound of the bird spray in the
wing, being the wing of the sound, bird, being where you are,
being all, and the water is the shallow of the sound inside
the bird, a shadow in the window of the man,

where is the bird that is the stop watch in the street, where is
the sky that is the bird sound that is sound, where is the
shallow where I dreamed about myself, up, between the clouds,
and balanced on the clothesline, where the stop watch stops
the clouds, and all the clouds, shallow, filling up the sky and
from the window where the man did walk, that the man
did walk from the window, that the man did walk, near a
mourning dove, so attentive to the line,

look, up at the clouds there is not one bird and is not one heart,
but is the sound of the clouds which is the sound of a mourning

dove, which is where the window is, steep and near the beach,
where the bird turned, swimming,

and while it is still this, it is morning, and there is no
stop watch, but I think there is a bird, and here in the
shallows of its breast is me, inside a dream, beside
the line that hooks me in, hooked, into the
midtown rain, bird, the hawk that takes the buildings
where it is, you, library of birds, covering the land mass,
miles and miles of all the bird where the sun comes up,
and it shines against the window, and the bird rises
above it, in song, beside its train.

OLD

As in the old days
for the wolves who speak
because themselves are
old, in trees, silent,
in the trees above the
heads of silent wolves,
the old and silent wolves
in trees who there are
quiet in the trees that
are so old themselves,
the wolves who eating
soup from cans are old,
the cans of soup that
are as old as wolves,
and I am old this year,
older than the trees or
all the wolves, in their
houses with the heaters
and the stoves and t.v.s
and the cans of soup,

and this is my old song,
that the wolves sing
from the trees, that
the wolves have sung
in dreams.

THE SPECIFIC INCENDIARIES OF SPRINGTIME

Inside of my inspection house there are
things I am inside of lacking only linens
and the tiniest of birds, there are small ideas
of tiny birds and things they are inside of,
in the middle of the small ideas of genius
we began inside of sundown,

I am hiding from relationships of springtime
in the tiny rooms with tiny birds, and there
are functions of relations, there are springtimes,
there are tiny birds and checkbooks and some
farmteams,

I am wanting only lemons where you have
wanted only linens in the center of the room,
I am waking up in long corroded rooms,
near Bakersfield and farmteams, in the vivid
dreams of rain, having dominion over these
animals and the salesmen on an island in

relationships with shepherd girls who carry
soft umbrellas,

Toward sundown, let me say that I am in
your absence forced to read a smallish book,
to read ideas of farmteams in the twilight
in the spring, where on an uninhabited
island I strangled all the shepherd girls and
then became a smallish book, and doused
the bed with kerosene he sleeps in doused
with birds and twilight books I dreamt of in
relations of the springtime that I dream,

Of farmteams, clearly let me say of sheep
and clearly let me say of spring in Bakersfield,
where I have strangled all the sheep and
several shepherds, where to read ideas
of twilight in a book, today, to a new love,
where in briefly retouched currency, functions
of inspections in the house now lacking lemons,
here I strangled all the shepherd girls and birds,
Where I read ideas of twilight to a newer love,

where the genius of liberty we began in the
middle toward sundown was a smallish bird
in spring outside of Bakersfield, where,
on an uninhabited island, to the twilight
of this genius in the book, to the mouthpiece of
the smallest sunlit bird, of the farmteam in
corroded blue relations, of ideas and in
inspection blocks, of occurring in the middle
of the twilight, of the dreams of smallest books
and salesmen inside Bakersfield, of wanting
only linens having wanted only wicker in
the center of the room,

I am a soldier of this wicker chair, I am
brandishing a welding torch and drill,
I am the island with the shepherds and the
sheep, I am waking up in Bakersfield in
rain, in a long corroded room, near the
farmteams in the vivid dreams of rain,
and in turning in the kerosene being slowly
doused in fire, I am, toward sunlight,
strangled by a shepherd girl, I am a salesman
of the islands of this currency,

Of rain, let the farmteams in relations
with the springtime in the checkbooks
find the rain, corroded I am, wanting only
lemons, only linens and then you, let me say
that you are on an island with umbrellas,
that we are woken in a room of springtime
birds, that nowhere is a smallish book,
and in the twilight reach dominions of our liberty.

HOCKEY NIGHT IN CANADA

Oh Canada, you are melancholy today
and so am I, and here is the giant metal airplane
that fills the sky above the steam heat of my
dreams, beside decisions well between the
quiet that's between us

and also do you think of the hibiscus
on your roadsides, Dutch, like bags of carrots
still heroic wrapped in snow upon the tiny
screens that show it to you, particular neighbor
who breathes, alive, asleep, beside the surface
of the ice, upon the moon in silver deep.

ALTERED STATES

Put them here and put me in beside the
caribou and them beside the past and
put the little stars inside their heads
inside the place they are with all the
crank shafts out in space and pretty pins
of orange bird heads where they go and
also that the radio is where it still
belongs alarmed along the highway as the
bodies where they were inside the ground
and also on the water put the boats of
water let them row for days beside the
moon and next to other things less brave
put all the tea cups and the things
still left I never cannot name.

FROM "MY TERRORIST NOTEBOOK"

This is the beginning of my terrorist notebook—all terrorism all the time. I would have had to blow up the World Trade Center to get anyone's attention when I was a kid. I'm tired of being nice. Nice is out. I want to live in a cave with Osama and sleep on the floor of the cave. I want to poke people's eyes out with their cell phone antennas. Maybe I would feel better if I exercised more. Pretty soon I will run out of money and that will be the end of my terrorist activities. We have a situation here, we terrorists, in our caves, blowing up the rest of the many muddy mouses, swinging by their mousie tails over the heads of the mousie moms under the muddy mousie moon, don't move, and watch the mousie moon, you mom of mouse, now watch the mousie moon.

SWAMP FORMALISM

FOR DONALD RUMSFELD

As if they were not men,
amphibious, gill-like, with
wings, as if they were
sunning on the rocks, in a
new day, with their flickered
lizard tongues, as if they were
tiny and biting and black,
as if I was a hero or they were,
as if the they and these us that
arrived, out of the same blue
ground bogs, as if from my
bog that I saw the sun and
swam up to the surface, as if
the surface was shining, like a
lizard to embrace, as if the
random pain of lizard heads
on sticks were prettier to eat,
as if I didn't kill the plants, the
water, and the air, as if the
fruit and the sheep were all

diamond shaped and melted,
allowing in the sun, underground,
crowned, in shadows, in the
main dust, from the self same
main dust spring.

BECAUSE POEM

Because they ate the tomatoes. Because all of nature is obsessive and bad. Because all of nature in this region is obsessive and bad. Because the corn and the worm they are friends. Because the tree and the roots and the worm are all bad. Because the root of the tree is the friend of the corn in the field. Because the tree and the root and the worm and the corn are all words. Because the words are all friends with the worm and the friend of the tree. Because some words they grew up. Because some words they grew up smarter. Because some words they grew up smarter and smarter. Because it's time to cut the trees. Because they were tree-cutters. Because they were hungry tree-cutters in a hurry. Because they were careless tree-cutters. Because the trees were cut by men not snakes. Because the snakes all bit the trees and ate the cutters of the trees. Because the cut up cutters cut the crops with snakes with the big teeth. Because the trees all lived there too. Because the trees and roots knew harmony. Because the burning cutters knew the trees and hungered for the crops. Because the trees were tired. Because the eaten burning trees were tired of the cutters, corn and snakes.

ON THE SUBLIME

They loved these things. Giraffe, they loved giraffe. They loved the concept of the tapir. They loved him, wholly unnamed. They loved competence and they loved the dark metallic stapler. They loved to trace the trajectory of the armadillo. They loved to speak of plankton. They also loved the fog.

ON THE LEMUR

That they loved to go on unmistaken, that they loved
to not to be gratuitous or cry, that they loved the
fortitude of yaks, that suddenly they loved the whiskey
and the sunlight and the key, that they loved the corn
cow and the cow corn that it ate, that they loved the cat
food as it rolled across the floor, that they liked and
loved the coffee that was warm inside the day, that
they loved the sound of hail and what it broke, that
they knew they loved the river that was made where
people dream, that they loved the loins of lions and of
lambs, that they loved confusion and the tools,
that they loved the whistle of the evening train, that they
loved the drugs they dreamt they loved and took inside
the dreams, that they loved their pictures taken and the
sides of barns, that they loved all outer space.

GREYHOUND ODE

Go to sleep little doggie
while the moon is still foggy
and the wild dogs all bark
by the light of the moon

by the moon little doggie,
under streetlights so foggy
while the wild dogs all bark
by the moon by the moon

at the waters so foggy
little dog little doggie
go to sleep little doggie
by the light of the moon.

HARPERSFIELD SONG

Purple clouds of winter weather,
starlings flown into the heather,
deer legs upturned in the snow,
wind-blown cow fur, grass fresh mown

Heavy lifting, icéd bever,
blue skies ringéd blue skies ever
where the moon is in the sky
rounded planets stay nearby

Having hearts of mammal murmurs
streams and valleys no hamburgers
only green things in the hay
only quiet day through day

To the possums in the creek bed
spears of pines and underleaf fed
in the sunlight in the rain
underpass of what to say

To the sparrows high on tree tops
fly on sparrows through the hedge stops
bristle up and fly away
black crest heads point this way gay

What to do for you is write you
into this a word for word zoo
I and you inside the thread
of the vowels sad and red.

SINNING SKEL MISCLAPE

O sinning skel misclape thy lock
from frenzied felbred feefs
and longitudes of long tongued fuels
unpebble-dashed deceased.

Unpebble-dashed, unpebble-dashed,
Unpebble-dashed unrose,
up from the theme that random flaps
in news flash rancid hose.

A morning dress of morning field
redrenched upon the sun,
that reads the wobble of the
air, the weary cautious rung.

The red-black innards laid up bare
for all to see and spy
tradition for the form of those
belingered, cheerful, nigh.

CHRISTMAS PRELUDE

O little fleas
of speckled light
all dancing
like a satellite

O belly green trees
shaded vale
O shiny bobcat
winter trail

Amoebic rampage
squamous cock
a Chinese hairpiece
burly sock

A grilled banana
smashes gates
and mingeless badgers
venerate

The asses of the
winter trees
rock on fat asses
as you please

Be jumpy
or unhinged
with joy
enlightened
fry cakes
Staten hoy.

FIRST

First train first day first donut first
coffee first cab first avenue first one
sock and then the other first fifty-first
a dozen fifty-five first frog first stop
first winter tree of leaves that fall first
revolution of the sun first step toward
science first fish up out of the sea, first
eaten, first eater, first laughed at, first
killed, first receiving radio signals,
first to do this, first to do that, first
beyond the first star in the moonlight
with the fish gods in the moon, first
at everything, first thing written in ce-
ment upon the sidewalk, first thing set
in stone.

SELF PORTRAIT

Fifty-seven dollars and the four
cents I left on the desk in room 118,
not much else a half a cup of tea,
unfinished books, some phone
numbers, the Wolf Man, tenacity,
one cat, at home in Brooklyn
with the spiders and also 7th
Avenue, the basement of Macy's,
the L train, the hello lady at
the Korean market on 14th
Street, hardly any smoking of pot,
was thrown out of the Charleston,
have a wheely-cart for my luggage,
two tranquilizers, four Prozac,
minor elk viewing, movie stardom
and the greatest waves of
happiness this sixth day of July.

FUTURE POEM

Straight out of the Abraham Lincoln place
in the middle of a primary election year
which is snow inside the mind outside
the tree and on the screen and if I were
a cat I would scratch my ears
all day and wear a woolen shirt
and have a mate named Jimmy
and we'd float away in a beautiful
pea green boat that is just a dream,
like the old people say
out in their old poems out in the field
and we are busy up outside inside
our dreamscape with our boats,
don't bother me, Agamemnon,
I am busy with my boat.

WHAT I WANT TO DO

Normal shit
like a normal person
yo normal person
twitching
under the sun
carcass haven of
cats and dogs
crossword puzzles
have coworkers
yo
I can operate
a Xerox machine
have a
nervous spot
used to be eighteen,
was once born
a fan
uncovered
in the
kitchen window

go out and
live in the woods,
build a small fire
have a hatchet
and a rabbit lair
away from
police men, garbage trucks,
and under the
temporary moon,
yo,
and under the
temporary moon.

THE REAL

Red cardinal in a white pine
who doesn't believe in roots and
branches or that fragrance
lost on the page as it's lost to
the eye in the thick of the woods
in a song of the night—

O great bear, o little well house,
O cheeping beaked thing
Inhabiting my sleep.

MAN'S FORTUNATE FEAST

FOR MENDY

The fatigue of feast,
the umbrellas and the
suits and ties, the
thunder of it,
floating into panther
fatness full
the checkmarks
that accompany the page
the gluttony of flower prints,
the tight skin of the sterile pear
gone spawned, consumed,
in leaf

no more lamb chops for you,
no more scrambled eggs and greens,
no more aardvark statues,
no more American flags,
no more caterpillars to
torch out of the trees,
cut wood, dead wood,

white pine branches,
drooping cypri,
dog asleep under the brush
also gone,
sun gone in the gray
swimming hole a stage prop,
water from the creek
feeding agile garlic greens in May

whose wallet, whose welfare,
whose heart, whose feathers,
whose darkness is the
darkness of a missing bird,
a tunnel of mind, an income of
herbaceous bruise, who is
and who is not, voracious
braeken gone.

JOIE DE VIVRE

Of all people of all time in any category james joyce, of all fears of thunder and of dogs, of irregulantcy, of punctuation and of pigeons, of this of a water-window of eyesight, of figures in the night, of the addition of numbers in dreams, of the addition of numbers in waking ten times three, of dots and spheres and the satisfaction of bright tourism, of wormwood and wormweed, of miles, kilometers, and spectacles, of world markets on transversals of the feets of all the birds, of the fantasy of renovated words, of the fact of material barreling nowhere, of horse hooves ebbed and square.

FOR THE NATION

Inconsolable as I am,
as the trireme is
as the unspeakable,
the uneatable, and the
early morning drunks,
insolvable as the words
mind and civilization,
hopelessly romantic
as the poem or the
chicken soup, carcasses of
chickens torn to bits by
poets, carcasses of poets
torn to bits by war,
felicitations of holidays,
like they say, damaged
grammar and slaughtered
sheeps, shipward, toward
the category of massive
storm birds, of mind, of
misery, of the gentle familiar

phrase, totally bankrupt,
awesomely leaning leeward,
leaning lightward leaned
enclasped in bitter leaf.

THE OLDEST DOOR IN BRITAIN

O rare Ben Johnson, do you
not know strife? Have you
not got topping on your cake, no
holes inside your shirt? Are you
asked to be yourself in dark
inside the rain? Is your door
the only door? Is your dark
the only ink to see? When
sweet love reads you, do you
read him back? Have you
fluffed yourself enough to
fly up to the moon? What
wants you, Ben Johnson of
the heart? What stone lies cold
on you?

AFTER CATULLUS

FOR THOMAS

In the beginning
there was grief,
a garden in the
center of a city
lit in rose and green,
a quickening of the
air across the wing
of a plane upon the
tip of the Labrador Sea
there was gleaming
there, a torque
not finished or forestalling
there was the promise of
Paris's perpetual pomme
pressed in gold,
there was only the hole
in the heel of a sock,
the steam of a since in a
fore-flung damp hotel
there was nothing baked
or boiled there was a stiffness,

a whiteness, a heaviness of
limbs and chips and silvered
peas, there was
this about it—a dipping
of the sun, a singular spoon,
a grid of hymns buried
under the finances of
a pickled cork, there
was finally that sense of it,
pharmacies or chemists
or high streets or the shape
of an ear of a baby asleep,
heavily there was that,
let me explain it again let it
be turned by the heave
of a hundred craven wivers
of verse, let the pendulous
balls of finest quality lead
render it into what I think
it is. Let me go back
to that garden in the
center of that city
to know I who I loved.

AMEDILLIN COOPERATIVE NOSEGAY

FOR BEA

I.

Into the eve of a picnic of trees
    of the strawberry rugulet rabbit tyrone
into a glazed economic disturbance
    caused by the rain most dramatic and strange
    small whole moon in the sky   fishlike in semblance
    as damp as an amphibrach
    the anthony braxton gland of ant launch

    wind blown shutters   angry household gods
        wet september horses
    schubert's trout quintet   (shy franz schubert)
        two german shepherds
al qaeda in flushing   and *earth's microphone willy-nilly*

into the eve of   *multitudinous seas incarnadine*   all one word:
    shy franz schubert   yuki lily atkins
        feverish hippo zion   fallen giraffe incident

        and the mysteries:

christ, death, genitals, the stimulation phase, salivation of the lamb,
william partridge orange, boring dutch milkmaid, the paranormal
finger, seven west 46th street's aristocratic vagueness panda, tur-
quoise buddha henpeck pacification, fleckner sarkis bop, object
relations banana, offending purple snowsuit, pegma and plengg

> with tender purloined sunlight
> at winter's lip

> specializing in yellow
> starlings in flight
> over arthur's seat

> this very linty cow
> that useless tibetan babysitter
> the prime meridian a pale dead moose in the sky
> into the eve of a picnic of trees
> of the strawberry rugelet rabbit tyrone

tenemos par chinches
helen mirren naked running from what

> the wild screaming beaches of the ancient mariner, his dutch

husband and four mosques by the by an ermine trouser snake over
the rainbow of red meat hedonisms, get rich quick, lose weight now
pasha parker penguin

and on brick lane
a television fell
from a lorry
we bought it
for fifty quid

waves of sleep a lovely lincoln, albuterol, first snow

this state sponsored car alarm, my lost mason jar, the lonely bird,
autumnal burnings, duncan's, cold and clear,
while slyly coffee hangs
outside below a
wall of snow

on bodega dust: include emancipatory relationships, odyssia's very
original boobs and the warm apt facts of john thaw, ham, and train
stations, this moon dewed glass, this small moon, this ba ba ba (first

instance of) grandmother in grave these fleeting forms: very gentle
sikh, book of penis, italians in florida, and allen also

register individual mayweed, harvey, jack and bob, robert, jess, and
stan, anne's red noir, lonely frank o'hara, perpetual free actuaries,
almost actual giraffe, humorless minimalist electronica, very linty
cow, American medicated individualists

this plantain a modest garden, kate mcgarrigle also, three guinea
hens, very linty sunrise, four latin grannies and domenica with a
new calendar, lonely nina simone, very gray day, the case of the
missing stamps, a foot massagenist, and the creation of earls

leap over a
large rock splendored
with april moss

for the sea, sailing, and the french revolution, pines and pineapples,
gumming finger food and winter cress with weapons grade lit-
erature his fiancée jane sewing chickens together the sparrows in
the cherry tree, the hedgehogs in the chanterelle bin, locust and
bartelby: first two worlds, blender, air conditioner, guinea pig and

the pedestrian on queens boulevard, a wriggler, I, all of nature, an occasional seagull, howth castle environs, a pale dead moose in the sky, an idiot in cat suit, an afghan ameer, the persian empire and two mathildas

cher dumps me (in a dream) a disregarded entity in wiggim's forest, a tittie rizzle, after the z, after the e, a luminous simultaneity, silver and hearts prophet mohammed in a bear suit, an omelet corner, my actual entity, my baby bear, my presentational immediacy, my beach plum, in blue lobelia, for mary osborne, this year and the next that is scented vaguely of potatoes

there was too
much of lester
in that room

removed his caterer in the koreas

a ready-made world, salerno's water buffalos,
the lemon sun in the sky
the silver cat in the nepeta

and lewis's mother
william blake's mother
sun ra's space world
the sixth extinction
this, peter's banjo
that, allen's harmonium
what do you
know about chickens
about sadness and
raspberry jam and
the hundred thousand
songs of milarepa
a molecular empathy
plinkets of sunlight
connecting all the
stars

ray's gay baby, floating lunged at rhino, empty macho rhetoric,
female swordfish captain, friday interior enhancements, bebe con
queso with very many steps, very many g's, a weary charlotte prod-
ger washing birds while high on marijuana, beautiful gingko trees
here and there, toughest well ever, a something oxbow,

old fashioned hominid

yes, to have
a favorite place

into the eve of a picnic of trees
of the strawberry rugulet rabbit tyrone

contemplative roommate wanted: no snow globes, that new things
happen in the equinox with a baby named ellington, brad will's
laundry (in a dream) call me hester drooping joe-pye weed,

for her now
a wood mite
white sweet clover

pale dead tree in the sky,
the whirled imperfect

while bumble bees
breakfast in the
lamb's ear's stalks

own some land
have some trees
google in indonesia

(in a dream)

land of wheels   dominated by sycamores

we talked about fish for hours
faggots, pie, bacon,

then sudden rain,   forgotten monkey amber

the catalpa tree, filthy third-world playground, alder, hazel, pine,
an italic gait, an antediluvian world,

deep metaphysical fatigue
beautiful but stupid
and tuli also

that we slip
into and out
of the world

companions, mud, adversity,

two snow monkeys,
two rabid beavers,
poor franz kafka

these ancient macaroons
and huge victorian fairies

my baby bear
my gorgeous goose
my beach plum

an occasional lycanthropy mcdonalds
in leroy
with ghost-free rooms
white sweet clover
water of. night!

II.

Thomas, bring soap,
  a fear of chipmunks   the end of restaurants   bears in dumpsters,
        cucumber, apple, and mint

           on Friendly Street
           the honey bees,
           the ash trees'
             flash of amber

           around the corners of the day,
           a ghost arbor:
           October's aster shadows
             say Quercus Borealis,
             the leaf torn
             from its tit

first k sound,
    milk, apple, cracker,

  trapped Chilean miners in a
  spectacularly disappointing universe,
        peabok sea quay   peking duck house

a plodder, I
    a globular body
    derived from the
    voice of a
        bird, rock, ring

perplexed by sheep, *dance, art, owls,*

        the penguin listening
        to the gramophone

    dance, art cow!   *eat and dance!*

        of the emperor
        and his genitals

        of a hungry
        Oaxacan space dog

        of an under-aged
        Moroccan pole-dancer

    owl   *ice*   *owl*

a yam diva,
  sea lions, mongooses, alpacas,

        I keep a chart with stars, "heap" for "sleep",
      Portuguese cuddle-up time and Nancy Samstein's sheep
      (in a dream)

those Legends of the Jews, these Tales of Hoffman, A Newton Pip-
pin and Sally Heming's offspring, spectral electrical reindeer im-
peratives: walk, dance, eat, sleep, peep, turtle, rabbit, deer,

    the color of the desert
    reflected in the fatigues
    of an Ortiz

    the midnight milkless melancholy of an icy beaver oracle

    the case of the elusive tricycle
    the return of the quiche-eating moose
    a stammering king
    enunciates a k
    to a new throbbing congress

this mole, that badger, this rat, low blue lobelia in a dream where
someone died and left Elton John in charge,
an octurnal nowl
in a kite of neige

neck   fork   tail

this debauched kinesthesia
that big dream porn book

welcome to the land of Rodney,
honey, ennui, pie

nice   shirt   moon

a whispered "ah" of a funny red seagull

that it must have
recesses, a room designed such

the translucent gray Elkhart dawn-light of
Lori's colon, Danny's job, Karen's pedicure,
Karen's mother's cell phone conversation

no horse
no owl

    one minky jeoffrey link
    fourteen camelback locomotive ox carts
    a red maple Velcro mama
    and Gloria Wong's life coach

I see you, camels, I see you Copernicus triangle food odyssey,

that seventy-nine commandos
and a dog were involved

    that they blew some people up and down

        catch it!
        stop it!
        go there!
        I want to do that,

in June's white wet
lilt of leaf

have courage, Mr. Wang
have a big house, a yellow telephone, a blue car,
have *mango turkey boobie*

the first *why*, the first *what*, the *what that he's doing*, the *what
is that*, the *who else*, and *what happened are you okay?*

a wood mite
a cabbage white
I'll fly it away
and men say yay

and where is he? and where is she?

Michael, Rynn, kari,
Akilah, Brad, and someday Harry.

hydrangeas and helicopters
  grief its proper mode

"D" in "Death"
under the space between

"will" and "remember"

that it smells like the painting of a flower

a red flower
a pink kid
a blue dude
and pythons
eating strawberries.

ABOUT THE AUTHOR

Born in Buffalo, NY in 1967, Jarnot studied with Robert Creeley at SUNY Buffalo and later earned an MFA at Brown University. The author of four full-length poetry collections and the former editor of the *Poetry Project Newsletter*, she has also written *Robert Duncan: The Ambassador from Venus* (University of California, 2012), the definitive biography of the San Francisco poet. Since the mid-1990s, she has lived in New York City.

*

Lisa Jarnot publishes with Flood Editions. Established in 2001, and incorporated as a 501(c)3 nonprofit organization in 2003, Flood Editions is an independent publishing house for poetry and short fiction based in Chicago. The press publishes four or five titles each year, including first books, volumes by established writers, and reprints. Flood Editions is edited by Michael O'Leary and Devin Johnston and designed by Jeff Clark. For more information, visit www.floodeditions.com.

The state of the world calls out for poetry
to save it. LAWRENCE FERLINGHETTI

CITY LIGHTS SPOTLIGHT SHINES A LIGHT ON THE WEALTH
OF INNOVATIVE AMERICAN POETRY BEING WRITTEN TODAY.
WE PUBLISH ACCOMPLISHED FIGURES KNOWN IN THE
POETRY COMMUNITY AS WELL AS YOUNG EMERGING POETS,
USING THE CULTURAL VISIBILITY OF CITY LIGHTS TO BRING
THEIR WORK TO A WIDER AUDIENCE. IN DOING SO, WE ALSO
HOPE TO DRAW ATTENTION TO THOSE SMALL PRESSES
PUBLISHING SUCH AUTHORS. WITH CITY LIGHTS SPOTLIGHT,
WE WILL MAINTAIN OUR STANDARD OF INNOVATION AND
INCLUSIVENESS BY PUBLISHING HIGHLY ORIGINAL POETRY
FROM ACROSS THE CULTURAL SPECTRUM, REFLECTING
OUR LONGSTANDING COMMITMENT TO THIS MOST
ANCIENT AND STUBBORNLY ENDURING FORM OF ART.

CITY LIGHTS SPOTLIGHT

1

Norma Cole, *Where Shadows Will:*
Selected Poems 1988-2008

2

Anselm Berrigan, *Free Cell*

3

Andrew Joron, *Trance Archive:*
New and Selected Poems

4

Cedar Sigo, *Stranger in Town*

5

Will Alexander, *Compression & Purity*

6

Micah Ballard, *Waifs and Strays*

7

Julian Talamantez Brolaski, *Advice for Lovers*